AF344523

DREAMS
ARE ANOTHER SET
OF MUSCLES

DREAMS
ARE ANOTHER SET
OF MUSCLES

DAVID SHADDOCK

Introduction by Denise Levertov

IN BETWEEN BOOKS
SAUSALITO, CALIFORNIA

Grateful acknowledgement is given to the magazines and journals in which some of these poems first appeared: *The Fault, Five Fingers Review, Hanging Loose, The Harbor Review, Mother Jones, Panjandrum Review,* and *Peace or Perish: A Crises Anthology.*

"Dolphin to Man" was first published in *Whales, A Celebration,* Prentice Hall, Inc., Canada, 1983.

Book design: Ann Flanagan
Cover design: Mark Wholey
Endpaper photo: Tupper Ansel Blake

In Between Books
P.O. Box T
Sausalito, California 94966-1842

This book is for Toby Shaddock
1910–1986

and for Toby Furash

CONTENTS

INTRODUCTION

The thematic divisions of this book each represent distillations of David Shaddock's life—preoccupations lived with long and intimately. He is a poet who doesn't glance at an experience and skip on to the next one but, in the course of making the poem or poems that come of it, follows it through as far as it will take him—through years of honing a single poem or into linked sequences of exploration. Years of love and labor in the service of poetry. As a result, his themes (the prose poems included, though these *Ten American Childhoods* are presented with an ironic detachment that isolates them to some degree from the others) interconnect, whether he's writing of dolphins or of children, of a beloved woman or of the threatened earth. There's an osmosis between the sections, as between separate poems; they present, though diverse in tone and structure, an ensemble, a spiritual ecology. And this is due in part to the way his writing life and the other facts of his existence reflect one another: if he writes of the lively creatures of ocean it is as a swimmer and small-boat sailor, if he writes of children they are the kids he has known through working for fifteen or more years in a daycare center. (A male sensibility emphatically responding to the individuality of children is, incidentally, something rare in poetry. Poems about children by men have most often been written only about the writer's own offspring or as elegies for some one specially loved child; a focus on living children, and on the child as a person, is rare—and Shaddock's are among the first to emerge from a generation that, at its best, has broken some negative cultural patterns.) By the same token, the love poems do not exist in a vacuum but against the background of our common nightmares, common hopes and aspirations: the woman's a real woman, and his love and fear for our threatened planet is expressed in work for world peace as well as in the brilliant and powerful poems of the *Carrying Corpses* series.

To excerpt key words from the book's concluding poem,

Hacer, Machen, Fabricare, (a title which clearly resonates with the Japanese student's equation, recounted by Pound, 'Dichten = Fabricare'), Shaddock's poetry knows, and makes us know, that ''What we make / of this world / is infinite / and perfectible / But our ability / to *make* / is wholly dependent / on a finite planet's survival.''

—Denise Levertov

FOUND MUSIC

FOUND MUSIC

One cricket.
Thunk of windpushed
windowpane. You

asleep, face in shadow,
hair backlit by glow
of blue streetlamp.

I who would gladly
walk on cut glass
to be here

am here
now
for free.

KING

The 2:03 S.P. freight
the fog signals on the marina jetty
the cutting out of the refrigerator pump

lead me down into this silence.

Laws of physics seem as precarious
an explanation of my continued
existence on this one spot

as the shaman's elaborate mythologies
must seem to some scarified doubter
sitting around a night-still aboriginal campfire.

I do not know if the self is a literary creation,
a box of identity that syntax
glues up to hold the present in.

I do know that even as I enter
deeper into this silence
something in me asserts these words,
this sentence my continuing life speaks.

It feels now that I am born
to utter myself forth from this silence
as surely as a star of fuzz
bursts from a blooming eucalyptus pod:

> Haley's comet
> Blue-green thistle
> Down on my lover's lip
> David the King

A LYRIC

There is a woman in me
who leads these multitudes of self
down to the well.

One thirsts but pride
keeps him from drinking.
One drinks deeply

but is not satisfied.
A furtive third plunges
into the well and drowns.

These are not heroes.
There is no story
in their endless thirsting

nor in the fruitless
labor
of their comely guide.

This is a quality
of amber light
in the water

one tongue
touches
and would speak of.

Not I
this thumb
& fingers

nor the
puppet
they work

nor the voice
of the puppet
nor the story

it tells.
Not the words
of the story,

pulsed puffs
of air.
not not not . . .

The dissecting knife
slices bone, marrow
single cells

cytoplasts
molecules
quarks.

What
is
still hungry

affirms finally
only its own
appetite

is
waiting outside
the door.

GROUNDSWELL

These dreams are another set of muscles.
Do you feel them pull at the dark waters all night?
We do not know what shore awaits us,
whether thicket or inviting beach,
whether we will arrive bereaved
or reunited.

We study eschatology
and miss each little arrival
this stroke, that breath,
the moment of waking
when Eros finds again
his bride,
this body
from which first things
come forth.

Walking west across Jackson Hole
past Taggert Lake I come
to a place—lichen stained
granite stones and subalpine
fir seedlings rising
suddenly vertical from the plane—

I realize is the beginning
of the Tetons.

That these glacially flayed
peaks of 300 million-year-old
metamorphic schist
start here in a line
of loosely packed loam
I kick with my boot

thrills me.

I want this point
of actual demarcation
to suffuse my imagination,
to become for me a place—
beyond the preoccupied marshes—
where I can stand and begin
to let the world in.

HOMECOMING

POEM

Cock crows

the world is safe.

Mexico is

as is the smell

of cold braziers

and garbage. Toby

is asleep. God

has blessed us.

The sun

is coming in.

We are not worried

and will try not to worry

all morning.

THE FALL OF MAN

is evident
in the way you
scold me
for coming on
while you're trying to study.

Eros and Psyche
sequestered,
the former
greeted coldly
like a dripping beggar
at the aristocrat's door.

Yet it is of some
consolation that I,
chastened,
write a poem,

while you,
strengthened
in your knowledge
of suturing,
go forth to repair
the bottoms

of women
who give birth
in pain.

HOMECOMING

That the day's humdrum
hummed all day
like a breeze
through tuned wires of anticipation

that from the rush hour
freeway one car
peels off and finds
its unerring way to this door
where the nine has lost its top nail
and become a six

that it's your car, you
coming home from an all night call shift,
exquisitely grumpy and overwrought,
the blood of a birth
still caked on your green scrubsuit

that you're not hungry, not interested
in hearing my ecstatic protestations of love,
that you want Morpheus' ministrations
more than mine—

are the contingencies that lead
me to feel that there are no
more contingencies, that my love
could be no greater
than it is now

watching you in blue chenille robe
throw me a bleary kiss
and stagger off to sleep by yourself
in the extra room.

TODAY

I kiss you
and want
no more

than I already have,
brush of lips,
wispy glance

of tongues,
the simultaneous
release of arms.

The part of me
that wants to confess,
that wants to hear

your confession,
lies asleep
like the blond cat

curled in a white
alabaster bowl
in the window.

Mint tea steeping.
Afternoon light
moves across the floorboards

toward your bare
feet, your legs
draped over mine.

LOVE POEMS: HIGHWAY 395,
NEAR ALTURAS

1.

Hauling doubles
        all lights
                on a dark

California highway
        the semi's load
                is love

or toward
        a new proportion
                of loving.

Your absence
        from these hills
                we once shared

is a hone
        to my sense
                of them.

Dark red rock,
        sage yellowish
                in the light

of a gibbous moon,
        a lonely diesel
                night passing.

My heart
        grows permeable
                pierced

by every
        thing
                that moves.

2.

Rapid motion
        through a strong
                magnetic field

induces an alternating
        current,
                a systole

and diastole
        pulse of
                plenitude

and absence.
        Seen from Alpha
                Centuri,

the second
        nearest star,
                today, this second

I loved you,
        last
                night I

did not
        you wouldn't
                touch me right.

We stand
        on a crusty rock
                that spins

as it hurtles
        through dark
                space.

Our motion
        through a field
                induces current.

Seen from
        Alpha Centuri:
                I love you I

don't love
        you I love
                you I.

3.

Seven Sisters
          in the east
                    sky

lover you
          are infinite
                    space tonight.

I enter the thought of you—
          the lion curls
                    of your hair

the tenderness
          of your eyes and lips—
                    and emerge

hours or
          no time
                    later

complete
          with a dalliance
                    of star patterns

a darkness
          of hill shadows
                    a black

tunnel of loneliness
          behind a night-speeding
                    semi.

The thought of you
          reaches
                    the tips

of the hair
          on my arms
                    which grow erect now

as if waiting
          to be touched
                    by starlight.

4.

Seven Sisters in the east sky

strings of neckpearls
diamond facets cut by Dutch Jewish fingers
dew on spiderwebs
running lamps of night trucks
moons on the fingernails
of African children playing jacks
flakes of hard white snow
in the Christmas lights of Salt Lake City
coming, the flash of light
behind closed eyes
sparkles in the eyes of half-wit children

Seven Sisters in the east

the cells of my body
awakened by your memory
rising to feed like silver fish
in a starlit stream.

RUINS

1.

What are we, love
broken by the broken baby
we've lost, standing

uncommunicative in the merciless
jungle heat, having
for each other no

commerce of grief, no
new-made pleasantries
to trade in.

We dole portions of anger
out to each other,
hard looks upon waking,

daily agendas
mutually adjusted
to differ.

Upon these stones the Toltecs
placed the still-
beating hearts of the sacrifices,

a debased misreading,
Séjourné tells us
of an older Nahuatl glyph

for the bursting forth
of the heart
into spiritual blossom.

Whose obsidian knife
cut this baby
from your womb.

What ritual will sanctify
our loss,
stop

this turning of heart's
flower
back into stone.

2.

We walk the uneven
rubble-filled ground
of the *Zona Archealogica*

remembering who
wanted this baby,
who resisted.

Tiny red globular
flowers grow in the stone
mouth of a life-sized skull

carved in relief
in a low
ruined wall.

At sunset, on the equinox
we watch an undulating
shadow descend

the steps of a pyramid
to join the brightlit
serpent's head

carved at its base.
At every step
something from beyond

wants to speak to us
but cannot
make connection.

Over cokes, in the hot
palapa
you read me

the guidebook's
speculation about slaves
building the city.

Morley, I say, says
no, it was spiritual
fervor.

You seem
in an instant
distant, broken.

3. *Cenote*

Thompson paid sponge divers
in the Nineties
to dredge the limestone crusted cistern.

Found:

gold bells
children's bones
little mounds of incense.

4.

You wake, stop
me from taking
the motorbike into town

'tell me what you thought
this baby
looked like'

'like my father—
I hoped it could bring
my father back.'

5. In Merida

The stone seats
of the Zocalo
are S-shaped, we sit

face to face,
absorbing the dark
peace of the plaza.

Our glances
for the first
time in weeks

are not the punctuation
marks of unspoken
sentences. A beautiful

Mayan girl in blue
embroidered *huipil*
proffers flowers.

You place one
behind your ear, turn
to show her

but already
she has darted
back into shadow.

The bells of the seventeenth
century cathedral
ring out

in the thick
tropical air.
Nothing fills

the vacuum that forms
behind their ringing.
Our hands

touch lightly
on the stone
armrest, each

an emissary
from a universe
of separate pain.

A man approches. Politely
we decline a guide for tomorrow's
visit to the ruined city.

FOR THE DYINGS

There are so many little dyings it doesn't matter
which of them is death
—Kenneth Patchen

For the dyings
        are grace
                formed by our moving

out of peril
        into vanquished
                certainty

a space
        between the piano notes
                when the yearning

in your eyes
        meets
                the yearning

in mine
        and we are slain.
                It is a way

out
        so different
                from the annihilations

we worked
        on each other
                through lovemaking

yet it is certainly
        the death of
                everything

we have been.
        Waking—
                new lines

in your face
        hold me to
                you like wire.
Woman I love
        there is no mourning
                our deaths
this morning
        the rain
                breaks on the textured
hills
        a moment
                revealing
their flesh
        still
                manifest
as ours is.
        Tremors
                our hearts
stop
        at every
                beat.

TRUCK

EDEN

She drags her bad foot
from table to sink,
carrying the glass cup
with soft-boiled egg remains.
Runs a little water,
needs to sit down.

Her son once called her love heaven,
now he calls it shame.
There is no return, he tells himself.
He hates nostalgia, hates
the feel of her wet, aproned embrace
on his neck. But he is still
dissatisfied, still looking for something.

Light streaking in through stained
kitchen windows. Yellow yolk,
white shell, bits of cream-colored
challah floating in cloudy suspension
in a cup of fresh-drawn water
that yesterday ran in a Sierra river.

A memorial candle
puffs out at midnight
of its thirtieth hour.

The one-eyed
ghoul face it makes
on the ceiling

gone in that instant.

I am a fatherless boy
an assertion
that for me had

no shape, or shape
only of monstrous shadows
that haunted margins.

Why did I fall
in love
with loss

if not to be close
to you,
Father.

A hole
in my belly
is pierced

by the blackness
that leaps out
as the candle dies.

I welcome the invisible
fingers that thread
me onto this necklace

next to you,
Daddy,
in the dark.

FLORIDA

Yeeaw yeeaw yeeaw
squack primordial
aquatic vultures drying wet
paper thin wings
on bare-limbed trees above
the alligator swamp.
Five great white herons
stand graceful, still
and silent in the distance.

Blue are Buby's fluffy
slippers as she pads
across the gold rug
in Miami
for a *bissel wasser.*

Behind her on Washington
Street the Food Fair
empties of toilet paper
piled high in the arms of
Alter kakers scared of shortages.

In front the wind breaks white
into the green sea.
Buby turns the tap
and a vulture caws
an ambulance sounds
a heron takes off
someone has died
the water flows into a glass
and the 'Glades are drained 8 oz. more.

Buby takes a pill
and looks at the clock.

''I like the climate here in the 'Glades,''
says the Nike-sergeant who picks me up.
''It reminds me of Nam.''

Everyone going crazy feeling guilty and lying.
Everyone eating fast food and taking pictures.
Everyone driving Mercedes and crying in each others' arms.
Everyone is Jewish.
This one stopped writing and is going to lawschool.
That one has stopped painting and is working at a skating rink.
This one saw Bob Dylan in a liquor store.
Everyone is having a breakdown or has found a cure or is out
        rollerskating.
Everyone is lonely like my mother.
Some went to high school with Henry Miller's son.
Some remember seeing Steve McQueen in the Palisades on his
        Triumph.
Some take drugs in the bohemian canyons listening to the
        chaparral snap in the heat.
Some feel like steers in a Chicago stockyard caught in the precise
        crosshairs of streets laid out perfectly flat.
Some wake early and walk on the beach at Venice before the
        smog comes in, trading glances of tenderness as
        imagination's jubilation rolls in unobstructed from China.

TRUCK

On the occasion of your hundred-thousandth mile

1.

A red surplus box on wheels,
the company's logo
blacked out as condition of sale,
save the optimistic white italics
''All Over the West''
painted on sides.

My father's company,
they sold it cheap,
a gesture of guilt or caring
for his untimely death.

Forty-five thousand when I got it,
three trips coast to coast,
a dozen times hauling
two ton loads of cordwood

down from Jim Green's land
in Whitehorn to sell
in front of the Berkeley Coop;

brakes failing in Russian Gulch;
doing two threesixties
on blackice Wyoming 80;

the time by 395
when Jeff and Toby and I
had to bail out, unable
to sleep for three-year-old
Jen's unbelievably loud bottle-sucking;

parked on the high desert
doors open
writing all night
under billion-star skies;

the 487 times
I cracked my head
on the lantern hook.

2.

I'd hoped to deck you with flowers
when the day came
but you caught me hauling the garbage.

So it goes.
This innocence
we've learned

by coming to feel
for what is left us,
a moving, a process,

the weight piled up
in heavy numbers—
then suddenly

wiped out.

All zeros.

Trucking this far
to nowhere

to begin again
as an end
in itself.

THREE CHILDCARE POEMS

ZEEK SILVER MOON

1.

Your mother makes eggs
you don't want eggs.
She makes waffles

you're not hungry.
'Titty, Amber, I want
titty,' you shout at

pick-up time,
unweaned at three-and-a-half.
She tells me

at our conference
she wants to correct
the mistakes of her parents,

of society
'which doesn't allow
children to fail.'

You walk through this intricate
world of block projects
and sets of friendship

with your carrot-topped head
primed to shrilly self-destruct
the moment you are crossed.

2.

To be a little man
in your fringed suede
cowboy vest with its

shiny sheriff's badge and
mother's invisible instructions
tucked in the pocket

is a complex thing.
I remember the bitterness
I felt having to shed

my Davy Crockett pajamas
and go forth to the cold
indifferent playground.

But once, Zeek, in sixth grade,
in the grey marble boy's room,
I entered the sport of the others

grabbing the tall blond kid's
balls he shouted 'Watch out
I'm good at this,'

but I held my own
or lost
and found in his cruel

complicit smile
what I had been craving—
not to be cherished

but to be divided through
by this least common denominator
of pain and pleasure, this cruelty

we are all, even these bespectacled
Yeshiva Kids or these hippies,
washed in.

Isn't that why Zeek
you kick the cat
and months later

are still waiting for the savage
and comforting grab
of claws on your neck.

MARISOL

Redhead highcheeked
big-boned Peruvian girl,
delicate yet
no hint of frailty

how can I win you?
My Spanish exhausted after *'como va,'*
I've come to you,
given you space
to come to me, had
Juan teach me
'Eres tu mi amiga?'

you looked down and pouted.

Is it perversity that these crushes
go unrequited?
Do your three-year-old eyes
see my inner self,
desire-ridden, craving
respite, a touch
that would break all my bones,
Rolf me to original bliss,
a sunflower, you, Marisol
growing in the garden
I would return to?

No wonder you hesitate.
What if some eighteen foot giant
tried to lay all that on me?

Thank God I've got my poems.

EVIDENCE OF ORGANIC FORM
IN CHILDREN'S POETRY

The four-year-olds
ended by mutual consent
        (acclamation, but un-
stated) their wish poem
here:

''I wish a turtle made a hole then went into the hole and buried
        himself up''

as if the poem's
energy
had found the same hole

and crawled in.

A DOLPHIN SUITE

DOLPHIN

When the waves roll my belly sunward
I snap my flukes
and break free into the air.
Now I crash boisterously down through the surface
and dive to cool ultramarine depths.

Seawaves hit the shore and break into filigree
colors splash my eyes, refracted
through drops of seawater: red   orange   magenta.
There's a boil—smelt
or mackerel. I'm off in a flash to feed.

No need to multiply this into something greater.
No need to divide this
into something purer.
I eat, break surface and spout.
The spray tickles my blowhole
and lingers like a cloud in the light a second.
Waves lull me, ripple me fully
snout to belly to flukes.
Safe in their rhythm
I sleep.

DOLPHIN TO MAN

A Greek coin, lost at sea,
stamped with a boy astride my back.
Over a wave we arc. For the boy
the ride of a lifetime.

What is there on the other side
of wave? A trough a
nother. What mint, what discourse expects,
what hand grabbing expects—

but more waves rocking
and salt in his hair
and a belly-thrill
as we crest and tail-surf.

Where did the boy go?
He's trapped in metal
heavy, unbuoyant, in the shadows
of sea-bottom, far from the dance
of sun and waves.

What could they expect to buy
with such as this? What when
in the apprehension of that boy's ride
they had everything.

DOLPHIN TO THE AUTHOR

We know together
that there is only one sea.
We are 'a colloidal
suspension of salts.'

Do you feel
the brush of my flukes
in your lungs
as you breathe?

Our blood beats
with the sinical rhythm
of seawaves.

Our bride,
this world,
awaits us.

TEN AMERICAN CHILDHOODS

E.'s CHILDHOOD

Papa used to give her the gold band from his Panatellas. She'd put them on her finger and pretend they were married. He'd take her for walks on the lake or skating in winter. But the night he wouldn't come see her be Queen Esther in the Sunday school play she wept bitterly. A cousin by marriage, C., came to stay with the family until he got on his feet. He used to go into E.'s room and touch her. She liked it, that was what she felt bad about. To get rid of him, Papa gave him money to move to California. (He bought a bar in Arcadia.) Mama never forgave him, throwing money at a bum like that. She started hating him every day. Even after his stroke, when he couldn't move on his right side, she brought it up. E. married an accountant when she was eighteen. She left him for a jazz musician. Now she's with an art dealer in La Jolla. She likes watching a beautiful ''New Age'' woman preacher on t.v. ''Is it spiritual to be impoverished?'' the preacher asks. ''No. The thing called money is energy. Wealth is your right.'' They shout together at the end of the sermon, ''I don't want it someday...I want it now.''

O.'s CHILDHOOD

It doesn't phase me is what O. learned to say, listening to her mother's jealous carping as O. ministered to her cerebral-palsy-dying father. It doesn't phase me she said, watching her older sister withdraw into silence. It doesn't phase me wiping the drool off daddy's chin then going to fix dinner because mother was having another one of her nerve attacks. It doesn't phase me the mantra she used to roof over the awkward spikes of her own nerves, thinking of her father in the cool grave, wanting to join him there. Later, when she grew up, people would orbit around the phrase's gravity: her husband with his impotent fits of shouting, her fifteen-year-old daugher with her string of boyfriends twice her age. A laid-back relic of the Sixties, that's what her friends would call her. When she was sixteen she had a dream that was to come back again and again. The dream would slip in under her sleeping sentries. Her father is reaching for her, trying to tell her something, but she can't hear, even if she puts her ear to his lips. After such nights she would put the dream in a heart-shaped box at the back of her underwear drawer, before slipping on her suit of it doesn't phase me and going to face the world.

They held her up on their shoulders to see Pete, Robeson, one time she even thinks Woody. She went to a camp where they rowed and sang labor songs. She never saw her dad until she was two and he came home from fighting fascists. She hated him, hated the move from Grandma's in Florida back up to D.C. There's a picture of her shooting daggers at proud Papa, eyes flaring under golden curls. Her little friend taught her to cheat at cards. She liked that, she wanted to upend the whole family. But they grew too diffuse. They lifted the burden of ideals off themselves. Dad played the numbers and delivered bread. Mom worked at a Jr. High, had her two more girls, and kept up with her worrying. They put up with T.'s boyfriends, her abortion. It was like they'd been gassed. She married a doctor and helped carry his ego, then dropped it and moved to California.

L.'s CHILDHOOD

He must've had one, but you couldn't prove it by him. Other people claimed they had a childhood. But he has a hunch they just banged them together out of a couple of old photos and something they read in newspapers. What does he have? His "dad" smelled of lanolin hand cleaner. His "mom" smelled of hairspray. He remembers waiting. There were girls, but he waited. Modesto waited, too. Were his brothers waiting? The thought that they weren't now fills him with bitterness. Anyway, nothing happened. He left home and waited some more. He got into drugs. "Home" faded to a dot like the picture on old-fashioned t.v. sets when you turned them off.

J.'s CHILDHOOD

Was scientific and lonely. All he thought about was death. He was an only child and needed a brother, but there was no one to play with but death. At school he would be thinking about death while the others learned about dairies in the Our Neighborhood unit. Once in awhile he would stop thinking about death and try to catch up, but mostly nobody noticed him. His parents remembered the Depression and were very frugal. To J. the Depression seemed very important, a time when death was near. He was comforted that his parents paid it so much credence. J.'s father was a scientist and J. always had microscopes and chemistry sets. All his experiments were about death. His favorite chemical was Potassium Ferrocyanide. He would have like to kill one of his idiot cousins. But only out of curiosity, not malice. When he was sixteen he fucked a whore in Santa Monica. Then death came to him, all night by his shoulder, death death death. He flunked trigonometry. He stayed in his room awhile and then left home.

G.'s CHILDHOOD

He would listen awake in his room while his stepfather would come home drunk and beat and then rape his mother. G. was the only one in the family that his stepfather allowed into his basement workroom. G. would help him with his projects, like making an oak dining room table, finishing it with coat after coat of fine stain and varnish. G. liked everything about that but his stepdad's taste in music, which inclined to classical. G.'s stepdad was friends with all the cops in the precinct, and when his mom called them they would just come over and poke him in the ribs and laugh. Finally she left him and moved to California. G. went to live with his natural father. He tore up the place one night after his dad criticized him. The bill for the damage and the nine months in the bughouse was fifty thousand dollars. G.'s father told G. that he would have to pay it back, even if it took his whole life. The hospital said G. could leave, but only if he went to live with his mom in California. He did but then they couldn't get along. She kept nagging him about his heavy-metal radio. When he pushed her she called the juvenile cops and they took him to the hall. He likes it there, really. He was surprised to find there are kids like him there, not like, you know, heroin addicts or something.

M.'s CHILDHOOD

Her mom died when she was three and she moved about ten
miles off the reservation to her grandmother's shack. This was
North Carolina. Her grandmother taught her to make things.
When she was eight her grandmother said she had more things
to teach her, but she couldn't teach her with talking. So they
lived in silence and her grandmother taught her by drawing pictures in the sand. When she was eleven the school called the wel-
fare because she was so dirty. She cried and begged to stay, but
they took her to live with her German grandmother in Charlotte.
Her German grandmother thought she was possessed because she
wouldn't talk. She worked her hard and taught her to read the
Bible, which were the best things she knew for her. M. ran away
up north when she was sixteen. She met H. who was on vacation
from prep school. His dad owned a company that made stereos.
They took mescaline and M. had a seizure. She got pregnant and
they wanted to keep it. H.'s dad offered M. ten grand to dis-
appear. She refused thank you. They moved to Boston together.
But then H. got arrested during a riot on the Common for having gas and coke bottles in his van. Did I mention that M. was
beautiful? She was and she loved to sing. We stayed up all night
singing one time when H. was in jail. She had a high, pure voice.
Her favorites were Neil Young and Van Morrison.

He played inside mostly but when Dad was home on leave he played outside. Mom said they were going to Sioux Falls to live with Grandma because Dad drinks too much. Then they moved back. One time after Dad got his discharge P. got to be his special friend, helping him set up the new circular saw. But the guard rail was made wrong and flew off and killed Dad in the head. P. thought he'd done it to Dad because Dad was mean to Mom. He felt bad for awhile then kind of forgot. They moved to San Diego. P. had some friends and got B's. He always liked the beach. He met a girl in high school and they went all the way. Her mom put a stop to that. P.'s mom met John and they got married. John caught P. smoking pot and they kicked him out of the house. That was when he decided he should be an astronaut because he could walk through time. You see the thing is people used to follow Jesus and be good but now they need something new. I thought this rich guy in Newport Beach believed in me but then I found out he didn't. I know how to live on edible plants and shells. Do you think the library has books on sex change operations?

K.'s CHILDHOOD

He was born with three feet and a harelip. They cut off his extra foot a centimeter at a time. This took five years, once a week. Then they wanted to start on his lip but his mother was sick of driving him to the hospital. She decided she could do it just as good at home with the stapler. K.'s dad was always doing yoga or making money. He never heard K. screaming, but complained mildly when he found his stapler empty. K.'s mother got crazier. As the years went on her only worry was that someone would touch something. She forgot K.'s name and their only contact was when she screamed at him for touching something. K.'s father's wealth increased sevenfold. K. joined the circus and became a dog. Still disguised as a dog he joined a family of intinerent negroes who taught him to sing the blues.

MY CHILDHOOD

People came in, dropped off rage, and left. My father entered and snored to Gunsmoke. On weekends there was roast beef and we could really get down to fighting. *Tante* Bessie would knit and grow increasingly catatonic. The house sucked up dogs and cats and postmen who were never seen again. A Hell's Angel chased my mother with a sprinkler turner-oner. James Arness lived across the street. It was a high-toned neighborhood and we were terribly out of place. My mother would chase my father into the street with a kitchen knife. He would jump in the Pontiac and drive around and around the block honking the horn to taunt her. All the kids shook me down for my lunch money. At night, after bedtime

> I would watch the westerns
> through the slats in my louvered doors
> and dream of the infinite peace
> I could find in a real gunfight.

CARRYING CORPSES:
POEMS FOR SURVIVAL

VOICES OF THE DEAD
SPEAKING IN THE DARK

Where will we put them
If they all come at once?

Who will triage their anguish
Who begin them on the steps of repentence?

And no world left, no
New incarnation possible.

Only this multitude

    Weighed down by unlived life
    Lips frozen midsentence
    A syllable of rage
    Stranded on their tongues.

IN THE HIJACKED WORLD

We do not know when they will come for us.
We hear rumors of what it will be like.
Perhaps the seeming normalcy of our lives now
is the cruellest of our tortures.
We are allowed to write letters,
But who is left outside to receive them?
From the window we watch the bombs being loaded
and wonder how much longer our captivity
will be useful to them.

ABSENTEE BALLOT

This is no vacation.
The train sweating all night
and now no breeze through the slats of the *palapa.*

The hangdog expatriate next door named ''Crow''
wants to talk about the bomb, he's
not worried, he's a Buddhist and besides's
got land in Tierra Del Fuego,
last place he figures they'll hit.

This bore bores into me,
finding a hole that's already there.
Found a new friend, you ask,
back from your swim,
and my eyes flare up at you with anger.

The afternoon light shifts through the thatch
casting a varying net of shadows
on our separateness, you in the hammock,
dozing, me staring blankly at an attempted letter.

At night the town glows weakly across the bay.
A generator clicks on and off.
The tide receding over pebbles
takes our breath with it.

Where's the gold coin
I cached for emergency
the one minted
with a human, pitying face.

THREE ROLE PLAYS

1. BOMB AS BUDDHA

You sit, silent in your dark silo
Husbanding the concentrated energy of the cosmos.
You are no more destructive than we will you,
No more fearful than the fear we have
Of our own hearts. Your image
Flies like a prayer wheel in the wind of our thoughts,
Intoning a binary mantra of death and life.
Yet to you it is no matter
Whether you sit underground forever
Or burst forth in a few seconds' fury.
You are not violent.
It is our tight grip on this world that is violent.
To survive now, you say,
We must make friends with not-being.

2. BOMB AS MEPHISTO

Why this is hell, nor am I out of it.
                                                —Marlowe

One kiss of my white gloved hand
and the deal is sealed.
Now your eyes are my eyes.
Already your Gretchen
seems vapid and nauseating.
Already you see malevolence
in the eyes of the stein-clanking students.

Listen:

> So my dad just hired a backhoe and did it himself . . .
> You mean the same one who used to go out with Barry
>   Shimmel . . .
> It was just a cuntshair off, so I took some shavings and
>   shimmed it . . .

Those are the flatfooted grunts they marched to a bunker
a mile from ground zero.
Before you congratulate me on my handiwork
I must remind you that even with a hundred
rads apiece in them they're better
off than you with your endless questions.

Look:

> that's Everyman
> choking as he swallows
> his own tail.

I see you fix him closely
in the crosshairs
of your disdaining vision.

That's capital.
You've become a bomb
more quickly than I could have imagined.

3. BOMB AS JESUS

That time I came as love
and surrendered to your violence.

This time I come as implacable
talisman of heaviest metal.

That time I asked
you to surrender your violence
to compassion.

This time only compassion will save you
from the apotheosis
of your own violence.

It was said
that when I came again
it would be to judge.

Now your own hands
are on the seal.
I have given you
the power to judge yourselves.

THE WHITE TRAIN

1.

Two fifteen-hundred horse Burlington Northern diesels
pull the lowslung armored boxcars and shotgun-slitted turret cars
        of the white train
slowly out of the Pantex weapons plant in Amarillo Texas.
It picks up speed across the scrub-brush Panhandle
into New Mexico where the land begins to lift
and piñon pine and bush juniper appear along the tracks.
It whistles over trestled canyons that hide
green ribbon rivers twenty feet wide and a hundred deep.
White water rushes in Colorado culverts;
red soil marks the blasted cuts of the roadbed.
The white train crests the Great Divide
and flies down the Rockies into Idaho.
Across rivers by moonlight: Salmon, Columbia,
the Snake. Dawn finds the white train
in the fertile Polouse, breadbasket of the West, and on
across the dry sageland of East Washington.
An extra engine joins and pushes the white train
over the glaciered Cascades and down
toward Bangor at the head of Puget Sound
where black painted submarines are ready for it to bring them
the bombs they'll carry off and wait with.

2.

This is not a Fellini movie.
The white train does not glide by on silver tracks.
No mysterious gangway appears to admit Giulietta Masina
and a host of colorfully-scarved women.
The white train is not a piñata filled with penny candy.
No paper maché Paul Bunyon waits to axe it in half
and set the urchins scrambling.
No Ahab stands peglegged on the foredeck,
obsessed eyes peeled for the white train.
The white train is not the objective correlative
of our debased longing for return.
The white train is not the one promised in spirituals
for which faith in the Lord is the only ticket.

3.

Its whiteness is utilitarian:
easier to clean and check
for radiation.

Its whiteness is for safety:
people will stop at crossings
for a white train.

Its whiteness is the gallows
humor of some college grad
project manager.

It is white to please
some death-longing general
who wanted the bomb clothed in the color of sanctity.

4.

We are running ahead of the white train.
Our feet work in long strides
magically finding the distance of the ties.
We never grow tired of running
but can't find the strength to stop,
to step off the tracks.
Our racing hearts draw the white train on
into the vortex our fleeing creates.

5.

The white train is crossing the mile-wide Mississippi
        near Memphis.
On the Tennessee side eight Catholic protesters
kneel on the tracks in prayer.
The train slows to thirtyfive on the bridge;
the engineer sees the kneeling figures; wheels
lock and screech as he hits the brakes.
Seven jump away, Sister Dobrowolski stays
still, praying in the name of Jesus for peace.
The train stops two yards from her.
The others walk back in front of the white train and are arrested.

"HE BECAME WHAT HE BEHELD"

Pound, staring at Usura
donned his jackboots
to stomp it out.

Reich, poking
with stiff fingers
the emotional plague armor.

All of us lined up
like the soldiers
they brought in to witness:

> 'We were five miles from the atoll.
> I was watching a petrel
> through the glasses.
>
> Before I heard the explosion
> I saw the bird silently
> vaporized.'

CARRYING CORPSES

1.

The man walking the slums at 3 a.m.
carrying a corpse he found
is caught
between two fears—the fear
of being implicated in a crime
and the fear of indictment by spirits
for disrespecting their new one.
He wishes there were a deep pool
or fountain he could dump his burden in—

but the town is so dry.

2.

8/15: dream. I am carrying a corpse through a strange town.
It is Henry Wolff. I don't know what to do with him. I want
to just throw it down, but dare not. Waking, I think how
this dream is related to my work on this manuscript, these
poems carrying the burden of nuclear war, not knowing where
to go with it, wanting to lay it down and run. Frail Henry,
with his Tibetan bells his nicotine and his smack, half Buddhist
scholar, half self-destructive nihilist; his beloved Rimbaud
prophesied our writing would end here.

3.

The Teachers shouted

Drop!

We clamored
under desks
taking refuge beneath
piles of scribblings
and wrong homework answers

While the dread
imagined jets
flew overhead.

4.

Some wake full
          of the world's death
                    every morning—

Or rather they never
          really wake. You can see them—
                    the droopy ones

Their lips pursing
          accusations
                    they can't quite

Articulate.

5.

The man walking the slums at 3 a.m.
is plagued by a new fear.
What if he is wrong—
what if his ''corpse''
is just comatose. How
is he to know.
Why does this happen to him.
Why did he stop.
Why is he wandering ever closer
to the hospital.

6.

A taste, like metallic
synthesized garlic

left in the mouth.
Something still closed

this morning—no room
to take in the opulent garden

outside this window.
Not left-over grief

for Daddy's blue
stroke-dead eyes

staring up from bed,
or Aunt Betty's cancer-skeleton

hand reaching out under
I.V. pump to touch me—

not that but this
penetrating smell

from the dream, this undead
world corpse we carry

like a new grafted musk gland
at the back of our head.

7.

The man walking the slums at 3 a.m.
carrying the corpse he found wonders
what would it matter
if his corpse were alive.
Where could he go. What hospital
would believe him. Would they
understand his anguish, take
away his burden
or merely drift by
along cold neon-lit
linoleum halls, mouths
covered with surgical masks?

8.

Wouldn't it be nice to see
a bulldozer level this city
put it in a trashcan
and close the lid?

My God,
I've started thinking like them.
So that's what comes
of carrying the corpses
every night.

9.

The man walking the slums at 3 a.m.
is sure now.
His ''corpse'' is alive.
It's his old friend
Henry, he
recognizes him.

10.

Because we are swimming
        with stones
                in our belly

we must braid
        our voices
                into rope.

Because each passing jet
        unmakes our world
                with fear

we must weave
        our worlds
                together.

Because the future-dead
        if we fail
                will be forever beyond

''Weave'' or
        ''World'' or
                ''word''.

11.

Gloria, 8 mos. pregnant
wading the Tijuana
River. Laughing she tells

of almost losing her
Coyote. ''I no able
to walk so fast.''

The corn in the yard
of her green tumble-down
house in Oceanside

is high as the roof.
She survives no
husband, no Medi-Cal

no car for the 30 miles
to the hospital.
She will survive

post-modern literary
criticism, the death
of God and the growth

of the new right.
She will not survive
a war

between these two
alphabetical abstractions,
U.S., U.S.S.R.

In the time
of the sounding
of one of Henry's large

Tibetan bells
time as a human
dimension could be

no more.
We are carrying this knowledge
down to the well.

12.

The man walking the slums at 3 a.m.
wonders
what is the burden
of this burden
what the weight
of this mist,
breath of a still-living man
on a hand-held mirror.

13. Postscript

Torn out newspaper photo
posted on clinic wall:

Gloria, toothless, grinning
holding yellow hospital-blanket wrapped baby

''First child born
in San Diego County, 1983.''

HACER MACHEN FABRICARE

What we make

                blue light
                Sierra glacial
                escarpment

of this world

                glint of mica in
                exfoliating
                Borrego desert rock

is infinite

                Olympic rain forest
                breathing
                through moss skin

and perfectible

            Homeric epic
            Cabbalist magic
            formula, body
            of Jesus.

But our ability

                sword in the lake

to make

                chance arrangement of yarrow

is wholly dependent

                theory of relativity

on a finite planet's survival.

    This is the crux and joy of our endeavor.
Wholly dependent

                finite
        perfectible.

This book was designed by Ann Flanagan.
The text was typeset in Compugraphic Bem
typeface at Ann Flanagan Typography,
Berkeley, California. It was printed
by offset lithography at Braun-Brumfield,
Ann Arbor, Michigan in an edition of 1000.